THE HEART OF
THE GOSPEL

THE HEART OF THE GOSPEL

God's Son Given for You

SINCLAIR B. FERGUSON

PHILADELPHIA, PENNSYLVANIA

P&R PUBLISHING
P.O. BOX 817 • PHILLIPSBURG • NEW JERSEY 08865-0817

© 2015 Westminster Theological Seminary

All rights reserved. No part of this book may be reproduced, stored in a retrieval system, or transmitted in any form or by any means—electronic, mechanical, photocopy, recording, or otherwise—except for brief quotations for the purpose of review or comment, without the prior permission of the publisher, P&R Publishing Company, P.O. Box 817, Phillipsburg, New Jersey 08865–0817.

Westminster Seminary Press, LLC, a Pennsylvania Limited Liability Company, is a wholly owned subsidiary of Westminster Theological Seminary.

This work is a co-publication between P&R Publishing and Westminster Seminary Press, LLC.

Scripture quotations are from the ESV® Bible (The Holy Bible, English Standard Version®), copyright © 2001 by Crossway, a publishing ministry of Good News Publishers. Used by permission. All rights reserved.

Scripture quotations marked (KJV) are from the King James Version.

Italics within Scripture quotations indicate emphasis added.

ISBN: 978-1-59638-961-8 (pbk)
ISBN: 978-1-59638-962-5 (ePub)
ISBN: 978-1-59638-963-2 (Mobi)

Printed in the United States of America

Library of Congress Control Number: 2014936848

A GLORIOUS STATEMENT OF THE GOSPEL

My seminary education certainly did not prepare me for every situation I would encounter in pastoral life and ministry. It did not prepare me to respond to Christians here in the USA who put their Bibles into my hands and asked me to autograph them! In such situations I am also usually asked to add a Scripture reference. My default text for these circumstances is Romans 8:32: "He who did not spare his own Son but gave him up for us all, how will he not also with him graciously give us all things?" I have a very personal reason for using this particular text. But the broader reason for doing so is because it is surely one of the most glorious statements of the gospel and of the sovereignty of God's grace to be found anywhere, even in this great letter. The purpose of this booklet is to identify and expound upon the heart of the gospel as Paul reflects upon it in this verse.

I will begin by briefly setting Romans 8:32 in its context within the epistle. These words occur at the climax of the opening chapters of Romans. Paul speaks about the power and majesty of the gospel and asks, "What then shall we say to these things?" (8:31). As he has climbed this rugged mountain of exposition of truth, power, and the grace of God in Jesus Christ in the opening eight chapters, he is now looking back—perhaps to the whole epistle—and glorying in the triumph and blessing of the gospel.

Earlier on in Romans, Paul boasted in the joy that was his. He rejoiced (or boasted) in the hope of glory (Rom. 5:2), in his sufferings (Rom. 5:3), and even in God himself (Rom. 5:11). But now, as he has so thoroughly expounded the gospel of God's

THE HEART OF THE GOSPEL

grace, he triumphs and exults even more eloquently. In doing so he throws out a series of questions that seem to challenge all creation.

- "If God is for us, who can be against us?" (8:31)
- "Who shall bring any charge against God's elect?" (8:33)
- "Who is to condemn?" (8:34)
- "Who shall separate us from the love of Christ?" (8:35)

The principle question is, of course, the first one. *If God is for us, who can be against us?* The apostle obviously does not mean that the Christian is free from opposition. Indeed he catalogs the opposition that he himself had experienced—tribulation, distress, persecution, famine, nakedness, danger, and sword (Rom. 8:35). What he means is that despite whatever opposition may come to us from hell beneath, from the earth around us, from our troubles within us—whatever opposition there may be—there is no opposition that ultimately can stand against the determined, gracious purposes of our sovereign God in Jesus Christ.

As I read these words from Romans 8:31, I often find my mind drifting back to David Ross's father. David Ross was a childhood friend who lived on the same street in my hometown in Scotland. We used to play soccer together after school. David had the twofold advantage of having a father who left work earlier than all the other fathers on the street and, in addition, a father who earlier in life had been a football—I mean *soccer*—player. If David's team was down 2–1, 3–1, or 4–1 with five minutes to go before our mothers called us in for supper, he would call on his father! No matter what we did against him, nothing could stand against the power and the skill of his father. If David's father was with him, it did not matter who was on our side against him.

This is our position. That is what Paul is saying. This is the power of the gospel in which we triumph in Jesus Christ. There is in fact much opposition—we would be liars to deny it; we would be false to the gospel to hide it. But there is no opposition that is able to withstand the irresistible advance of the grace of God in the life of the believer because God is for us. But the million-dollar question for all of us, practically, is: *How do we know that God is for us?*

HOW DO WE KNOW?

One of the most obvious false answers is: "We know God is for us because he has so obviously blessed us in his providences. We can draw the conclusion from the present enjoyments of good things in this world that God is surely for us."

I am always cautious when I hear a Christian say to someone who has made a major decision in his or her life that seems to work out very well, "Isn't it like God to do that?" I am cautious because it is also like God to take our best plans, our highest expectations, and in his sovereign, still-gracious purposes, to turn our rocks into sand and our plans into dust so that we may learn to say, "Shall we receive good from God, and shall we not receive evil?" (Job 2:10).

Our ultimate confidence that God is for us cannot be found in our ability to interpret the providences of our own lives or the lives of others. But, according to Romans 8, there is one irrefutable reason for the Christian believer to be utterly convinced that God is for him or her. That reason is that he is the God who did not spare his own Son but gave him up for us all. And if this is the case, how will he not also with him graciously give us all things?

The cross, the Christ, the gospel, is the reason the Christian believer knows that God is finally and irreversibly for him or for her. In these words from Romans 8:32, Paul explains this conviction by means of three eloquent statements—first, describing the action of the heavenly Father; second, designating the experience of the incarnate Son; and third, expounding the logic of the Christian gospel. We will now delve into these three segments of this verse in an effort to reflect on the heart of the gospel and, with the help of God's Spirit, to apply this word to our own minds, hearts, consciences, and situations.

THE ACTION OF THE FATHER

Notice first of all what the apostle has to say about the action of the heavenly Father: *he did not spare his own Son*. If you think about it for a moment, you will sense that this is a profound insight by the apostle Paul. These words, in a sense, belong to the same category in teaching us about the mind of the Father as Philippians 2:5–11 does in teaching us about the mind of the Son. The mind that was in Christ was this: he did not count equality with God a thing to be grasped, even though he was in the form of God. The mind of the Father, analogously, with a view to the same saving grace, was this: although the Lord Jesus was his Son, and in the very form of God, the Father would not spare him.

Unsparing

The fact that the Father did not spare his Son can be seen to be true simply in terms of the whole course of the incarnation. Paul has already stated that Jesus was not spared entering into, and taking to himself, the likeness of sinful flesh, nor was he spared coming for sin so that sin might be condemned in the flesh (Rom. 8:3–4). The Son was not spared the necessity of entering among us as an embryo utterly dependent upon the nourishment of his mother. He was not spared the agonies of the wilderness temptation when he was assaulted by the Devil—Son of God though he was. He was not spared the shame of nakedness and the awful humiliation of crucifixion. He was not spared the ignominy of his lifeless body being taken by two men, Joseph of Arimathea and Nicodemus, as a dead weight into the garden tomb. In all this our Lord Jesus, although he was God's beloved Son, was not spared the absolute helplessness of his humanity in his penal death. The author of Hebrews takes pains to affirm this humanity from which the Son was not spared, writing that the Son, facing the reality of his humanity and impending crucifixion, called out "with loud cries and tears, to him who was able to save him from death" (Heb. 5:7).

And yet the apostle is not thinking only in general terms about the way in which the Father did not spare his Son in the incarnation. Here in Romans 8 he seems to be meditating on the Son's sufferings as the fulfillment of Old Testament prophecy—specifically the sacrifice of Isaac and Isaiah's Servant of the Lord.

The Echo of Mount Moriah

The first Old Testament echo of the Father who did not spare his own Son is the story of the binding of Isaac in Genesis 22. As Abraham was taking his son up Mount Moriah, in obedience to the Lord's command to sacrifice him, Isaac asked this question, "Where is the lamb for a burnt offering?" (Gen. 22:7). Running through the narrative is the poignant motif that Abraham is being called not to spare, but to sacrifice, the son whom he loves, his only son, the son of God's promise (Gen. 22:2, 16). In Romans 8, Paul picks up this language and embeds it into his understanding of how the gospel ultimately fulfills the Abrahamic covenant promise.

Abraham essentially said to Isaac, "Depend on the promise that God himself will provide a lamb for the sacrifice" (see Gen. 22:8). Yet as the story unfolds, we notice that, in this particular incident, what was provided was not a lamb, but a ram (Gen. 22:13). Throughout the days of the Old Testament, God's people were left asking the very same question that Isaac himself had posed to his father, "Where is the lamb for the sacrifice?" . . . until one day John the Baptizer stood on the banks of the Jordan and cried out, "Behold, the Lamb of God, who takes away the sin of the world!" (John 1:29).

The echo of this language here in Romans 8 underlines what the apostle Paul is saying to us: "Do you not see this principle? The Father who permitted Abraham to *spare* his son was the Father who was able to do so because he had resolutely committed himself to the *not sparing* of his own Son."

The Echo of the Servant of the Lord

As Paul continues in verse 32, he echoes one of the great Servant Songs from the latter half of Isaiah. There, in the songs of chapters 42, 49, 50, and 52–53, Isaiah puts into the mouth of our Lord Jesus, as it were, a predescription of his experience. He became the one who would be the Lamb which God would lead to the slaughter (Isa. 53:7). Isaiah's words became so fully our Lord's:

> The Lord GOD has given me
>   the tongue of those who are taught,
> that I may know how to sustain with a word
>   him who is weary.

> Morning by morning he awakens;
>> he awakens my ear
>> to hear as those who are taught.
> The Lord God has opened my ear,
>> and I was not rebellious;
>> I turned not backward.
> I gave my back to those who strike,
>> and my cheeks to those who pull out the beard;
> I hid not my face
>> from disgrace and spitting. (Isa. 50:4–6)

And then Isaiah goes on to use language that is echoed in the rest of Romans chapter 8:

> But the Lord God helps me;
>> therefore I have not been disgraced;
> ....
> Who will contend with me?
> ....
> Who is my adversary?
> ....
> Behold, the Lord God helps me;
>> who will declare me guilty? (Isa. 50:7–9)

In the very manner in which Paul draws on these two great strands of Old Testament prophecy and typology about the Lord Jesus, he is seeing the way in which this principle has been embedded in all the Scriptures: *God, who is our Father, is the kind of God who for our sakes and in fulfillment of his covenant promise, did not spare even his only Son.*

So far we have seen that God the Father did not spare his only Son in the incarnation. We have also seen the very specific way in which God fulfilled his prophetic promises by not sparing his only Son. But perhaps the most remarkable aspect of the unsparing action of the Father is that God did not spare his only Son despite the fact that the Son *asked* that he might be spared.

The Request to Be Spared

The Gospels record that Jesus *asked* to be spared: "Abba, Father, all things are possible for you. Remove this cup from me" (Mark 14:36). We might first ask why Jesus prayed to be spared the cup. After all, some Christian martyrs have gone unflinchingly and almost eagerly to their death. Why does Jesus ask to be spared? The answer is that he uniquely understood what was in the cup his Father was giving to him. He saw the judgment, alienation, disgrace, and shame of which the prophets had spoken poured into that cup. He knew it was the cup of God's wrath (Isa. 51:17–22; Jer. 25:15–17; Ezek. 23:31–33; Hab. 2:16).

Jesus understood what he was about to experience as he went from Gethsemane to Calvary and to the death of the cross. It was nothing less than entry into a sphere where the great covenant of God and the Aaronic benediction would no longer function. He was going into territory where there was no peace, where he would no longer feel the promises of Psalm 23. He was entering territory where his cup would run over, not with blessing but with the divine curse, and where his glory would be covered with shame. No wonder, then, as our Lord ponders the cup of covenant cursing, which he is about to take from his Father's hands, having already given his disciples the cup of covenant blessing (Mark 14:23), that he prays there might be some other way than drinking the dregs of the cup of cursing. He asked to be spared. We are on the most sacred of soils when we listen to the Savior's prayer in this respect.

And yet our Lord Jesus Christ *must* ask to be spared. He must for the simple reason that it is altogether and utterly inappropriate for the perfectly holy Son of God, clothed in our humanity, to ever desire anything but the unclouded smile of his Father in heaven. To be willing for anything else would, at one level, be a betrayal of his relationship with his Father. Jesus surveyed the prospect of crying out on the cross, "My God, why am I forsaken?" with the mind, will, and emotions of an unsullied humanity that longed, flesh and soul, for the living God. No wonder his soul was troubled and sorrowful (Mark 14:33–34)! The Son of God in holy humanity *cannot* be naturally willing to be separated from the smile of the heavenly Father. Indeed he *must not* desire it, for that would be an unholy desire—every holy instinct must rise against it!

Here, in the garden of Gethsemane, is perhaps the deepest clue we are given as to how the holy, harmless, separated-from-sinners Son of God could ever face real temptation. For here he is called upon to do what is utterly unnatural—indeed from one perspective, repugnant—to the holiness of the humanity that he has assumed. Yet, if we are to be saved, Jesus, who can never naturally will or desire to be separated from the smile of the Father, must bow his holy will to the Father's will for him as the mediator of the new covenant. The incarnate Son of God must bow his holy human will in utter obedience to the will of the Father—the will to bear our sin. So it is because of his own nature and the nature of the cup that Jesus *must* ask to be spared.

The Love of the Father

But the other side of this relationship between these two persons of the Godhead is that while the Son *must* ask to be spared, the Father *must not* spare him. Dare we even say the Father *cannot* now spare him? This is not a matter of naked power, nor is it a limitation on divine omnipotence, rather these two, Father and Son, have together entered into a bond and pledge for our sakes, in which they have covenanted to do what is, in its own nature, repugnant to them both.

In one sense, everything in our Lord's life was a preparation for his Father's refusal to spare him. He freely took our humanity and submitted throughout the whole course of his ministry to the will of his Father. Can you not hear him? "Morning by morning he awakens me. My ear is open to listen to his voice. What I say is what I hear my Father say. What I do is what I see my Father do" (see Isa. 50:4–5; John 14:24; 5:19).

In that covenant of commitment between the Father and the Son, few words can express their bonding together for our salvation. The Son was committed to the Father, the Father consciously present with the Son "until (in that humanity) death do us part." Now as Jesus reaches up to the Father and says, "Father, if it is possible, find some other way," the Father replies, "My Son, we promised. It is a promise 'until death do us part' under its curse. I know it is not possible for you, in holy humanity, to desire this alienation from me. Nevertheless, in your love for and obedience to me, bow to that which is against all of your holy instincts, and do it because you are the mediator. I will not spare you—that is our covenant bond for the salvation of sinners."

I have three sons, and my instinct would be to spare each of them. Is this not the instinct of every father? God had one Son, but he did not spare him. In his poignant book *Lament for a Son*, Professor Nicholas Wolterstorff describes his feelings and struggles following the death of his son in a climbing accident. There is a sentence in that book in which he reflects on how this single event has redefined his identity. I borrow it to help us to think about God. Professor Wolterstorff says something like this: "Now if anybody wants to know who I am, that person must learn that I am a man who lost his son."[1]

If we want to know who God is, which is what Paul is talking about when he describes him as "[the God] who . . ." (Rom. 8:32), we need to know that he is the kind of God who defines himself in this unique way: *I am the God who did not spare his own Son for you.* Paul here speaks about the wonder of the atonement from the perspective of the Father. What did our salvation mean to the heart of the Father? Not sparing his Son—that is what it meant: That is who he is. That is what he does for you. That is the kind of God he remains for you.

THE EXPERIENCE OF THE SON

But Paul does not end his statement of the heart of the gospel here. He continues on in Romans 8:32 by speaking about the wonder of the atonement from the perspective of the Son. From the perspective of the Father, the cross climaxed the way in which he was unsparing with respect to his incarnate Son. From the perspective of the Son, the cross was the climax of an event in which his Father "delivered him up" (KJV).

We have seen how these verses in Romans 8 echo the language of the Old Testament Scriptures. They also echo the language of the Gospel tradition, which Paul was presumably familiar with in oral or written form. In fact, this terminology of being "delivered up" runs throughout the passion narrative. The Synoptic Gospels use it to record how Judas delivered

---

1. Nicholas Wolterstorff, *Lament for a Son* (Grand Rapids: Eerdmans, 1987).

up Jesus to the Jews, how the high priest delivered up Jesus to Pilate, and how Pilate delivered up Jesus to the Roman soldiers in order to be crucified (Mark 14:10; 15:1, 10, 15). The phrase "deliver up" (or "hand over") runs through the closing chapters of the Gospels like a refrain. Paul picks it up here in Romans 8:32 as he describes the experience of the Son: he was delivered up for us all.

The Substitute Who Was Delivered Up

This is, first of all, judicial language—it describes a legal process. Despite all the ways that our Lord's trial was illegitimate and illegal, it was at least outwardly a legal procedure in which due process was supposedly taking place. Paul is underlining by the language he uses that the death of our Lord Jesus is not to be thought of in merely general terms—it was specifically penal.

Yet as Paul's traveling companion and friend Luke describes this amazing transaction in his passion narrative, he records witness after witness pointing to Jesus and saying over and over and over again, "He is not guilty. He is innocent. He has done no wrong. We have found nothing wrong with this man. Surely this man was innocent" (see Luke 23:14–15, 22, 40–41, 47). How can this be that the innocent one is being condemned? It seems that Luke himself is weaving into the very passion narrative the clues to help us answer this question. While Jesus' sufferings on the cross are judicial, they are also substitutionary. He was delivered up "*for us all*" (Rom. 8:32).

The crimes for which our Lord Jesus was crucified were twofold: blasphemy and treason. These are the very crimes of which Adam stood guilty before the judgment seat of God—blasphemy in that he sought to make himself equal with God, and treason in that he had rebelled against the lawfully constituted authority of God, the Great King. For this reason, as he stood in our place, our Lord Jesus Christ was arraigned and accused of the crimes of Adam—which are also our crimes. They are your crimes and my crimes in that we too have made ourselves, in Archbishop William Temple's expression, "in a thousand different ways the center of the universe." We have dethroned the King and rebelled against his lawfully constituted authority.

Before God's judgment we are condemned for our crimes. We can have nothing to say; there can be no special pleading: "No one does good, not even one.... so that every mouth may be stopped, and the whole world may be held accountable to God. For by works of the law no human being will be justified in his sight" (Rom. 3:12, 19–20). That is the reason why Jesus fulfills the prophecy of Isaiah 53: "Like a sheep that before its shearers is silent, so he opened not his mouth" (Isa. 53:7). Why so silent? Why not plead innocence? Because the Lord Jesus stands in the place of guilty and condemned sinners:

> In my place condemned he stood,
> Sealed my pardon with his blood.[2]

But Paul's words contain an even more mysterious reality. Our Lord's death—his being "delivered up"—is judicial and substitutionary. He died a substitutionary death as the result of a judicial process. But Paul also wants to emphasize that this judicial and substitutionary event also contained an element that was *paternal*. It was *his Father* who did not spare him.

---

2. Philip Bliss, "Man of Sorrows! What a Name," *The Trinity Hymnal* (Suwanee, GA: Great Commission Publications, 1990), no. 246.

The Father Who Delivered Him Up

In his recently reprinted study of Romans chapter 8, Octavius Winslow asks the question, "Who delivered up Jesus to die? Not Judas, for money; not Pilate, for fear; not the Jews, for envy; but the Father for love!"[3] I want to stress to you how important it is that we understand that the death of Christ is not simply an event that fulfills marvelous patterns of Old Testament theology. Our concern here is not merely the weaving of the intricate designs of Old Testament typology. *The cross—the atonement—constitute something that happened between a Father and his Son.* It is the person of the incarnate Son who dies in our place.

Remember that on the Day of Atonement two goats were set apart (Lev. 16:7–10). One was killed as a sacrifice, but the other had the sins of the people confessed over it and was then taken into the wilderness by someone who was ready. There the goat was set free to wander with the sins of the people on it. Just as there was no one else who was fit or ready to take Isaac up Mount Moriah except Abraham, his father, so only God the Father was fit to take our Lord Jesus by the hand to Calvary. We sing sometimes that "there was no other good enough to pay the price of sin."[4] But it is also true there was no other worthy to take his hand and to lead him up to the cross on Calvary's mountain.

We also sometimes sing, "One day they led him up Calvary's mountain."[5] But there is a deeper truth: "One day *he—the Father*—led him up Calvary's mountain." That is what Paul

---

3. Octavius Winslow, *No Condemnation in Christ Jesus* (Carlisle, PA: Banner of Truth, 1991), 361.
4. Cecil Frances Alexander, "There Is a Green Hill Far Away," 1848.
5. J. Wilbur Chapman, "One Day He's Coming," 1910.

is speaking about. He is saying that while the atonement took place *geographically* at Calvary—which incidentally was on the edges of Mount Moriah (Gen. 22:2; 2 Chron. 3:1)—and while it took place *historically* around AD 30, the atonement also took place *personally* between the two persons of the Trinity, Father and Son, in the power of the third person, the Holy Spirit (as Hebrews 9:14 tells us).

You see, Christ did not enter into a sanctuary that was made with hands, but he passed through the heavens (Heb. 9:24). In a way beyond our grasp, on the cross even as Jesus cried out with a sense of God forsakenness, he was in the Father's bosom (John 1:18). And in the Father's bosom he was effecting a legal, substitutionary, and personal transaction that had been planned from all eternity: the sins of his people were laid upon him, and the curse of God fell upon him. Consequently the blessing promised through Abraham to the Gentiles flows from the cross—from Christ's wounded side—by the power of the Holy Spirit to all those throughout the world who would come to believe in him (Gal. 3:13–14).

The Giver and the Given Up

We must be very clear that it is not redemptive history that died on the cross for us. It was not typology that died on the cross for us, nor systematic theology, nor preaching, nor the sacraments. It was the *person* of the Son of God in our humanity who died on the cross in an inner-Trinitarian transaction of grace between himself and the Father. He bore the holy curse of God upon his soul and prayed, "Father, forgive them" (Luke 23:34).

I sometimes reflect quietly on the Lord's words on the evening before his crucifixion when he told his disciples to refrain from violence: "Do you think that I cannot appeal to my Father, and he will at once send me more than twelve legions of angels" (Matt. 26:53)? I imagine those chosen angelic witnesses of our Lord's passion and crucifixion returning to heaven and veiling their faces like those creatures in Isaiah 6. But they do not now cry, "Holy, holy, holy." Rather, they cannot look at the Father who has turned his gaze away from his own Son in our humanity. What can angels say to the Father at this moment—to him who in his heart must know more deeply than King David the cry, "O my son . . . my son, my son . . . my son, my son" (2 Sam. 18:33)? Do you not think that if David tasted such depths of pain, then the heavenly Father (in whose image even fallen David still remains) must have willed for himself to enter depths of pain beyond our understanding?

True, our theology tells us that God is never the passive victim. He is in that sense "without . . . passions" as the Westminster Confession says.[6] But that is not to say he is a lifeless monad. Rather, whatever he experiences he does so not as a helpless prisoner but as a willing participant. If David, the king and image of God, can plumb the depths of pain, then the One whose image he is surely does so as well. He has given his own Son to die for you. He knows:

> There was no other good enough to pay the price of sin;
> He only could unlock the gate of heaven, and let us in.[7]

I sometimes wonder if among those twelve legions of angels there was one angel who had the memory to recall and the insight to quote to the others what their Lord had once

---

6. The Westminster Confession of Faith 2.1.
7. Alexander, "Green Hill Far Away."

said: "*The reason* the Father loves me is because I lay down my life; I lay down my life for the sheep" (see John 10:15, 17). *Thus the very moment of the alienation of the Son, in our humanity, for our sake, was the moment of the profoundest depths of his Father's love for him.* I can think of no better way to describe this moment than in the words of another hymn. The Father looks at his humiliated Son upon the cross and says, "If ever I loved thee, my Jesus, it is now."[8] He stands like a Father who has watched his Son go into battle and says, "That is my boy! My Son is doing all of that in obedience to me!"

So Paul speaks about the atonement, the heart of the gospel, first from the perspective of the Father who did not spare his Son and then from the perspective of the Son who was delivered up for us all. But Paul goes one step further in Romans 8:32—he gives us these two perspectives to give us a third one.

THE LOGIC OF THE GOSPEL

Let me try to take Paul's further step by pointing out where he is going with this. The action of the Father was unsparing. The experience of the Son was that he was delivered up. But Paul has been saying all of this in order to make a personal, practical, and pastoral point. It is so characteristic of Paul that the highest and deepest theology has a practical, pastoral goal. Now, at the end of Romans 8:32, he develops a simple syllogism: if God has done this for me, then I can be sure that he will give me all things.

Paul communicates something wonderful here about the truth of the gospel. What he says can transform our Christian

---

8. William R. Featherstone, "My Jesus, I Love Thee," 1864.

lives and deal with our deep-seated needs, which keep unfolding from the depths of our being and which so often give rise to a mistrust of the Father. Paul is arguing that the fruit of Christ's death on a tree reverses the fruit of the death that came from another tree. But there is even more than that! The fruit of the liberating *truth* enshrined in this death on the tree of Calvary is the ultimate antidote to the *lie* that caused death to come from the tree in the center of the garden of Eden in the first place.

Remember that God set Adam in a garden surrounded by lavish plenty, but the Serpent hissed, "Has God said that he doesn't want you to have any of this fruit?" That was a word from hell, and we have not escaped its echoes and implications reverberating in our own hearts and lives. Some of us hear it daily: "God doesn't really want to do you good. Look what's happening in your life. He doesn't really love you." Here, in this great statement of the gospel, Paul provides the medicine for this deep-seated sickness in your soul. If he did not spare his own Son for you, then you can be absolutely sure that the Father will stop at nothing to bless you, keep you, guide you, lead you, and bring you to glory.

> And when I think that God, his Son not sparing,
> Sent Him to die, I scarce can take it in,
> That on the cross, my burden gladly bearing,
> He bled and died to take away my sin.

It is only then that the Christian begins to sing:

> Then sings my soul, my Savior God, to thee:
> How great thou art! How great thou art![9]

---

9. "How Great Thou Art," translated from the Russian by Stuart K. Hine, 1949.

This is the heart of the atonement. The Father did not spare his own Son. He delivered him up for us all. Because he has done that, the apostle Paul knows that no opposition against him can stand. No accusation can stick; no condemnation can destroy. No separation can ever tear us away from the love of God in Jesus Christ our Lord. This is the power of the truth of the gospel in us.

Do we trust God as this kind of Father to us? Can you not trust this kind of God and Father? Do you love him? Do you think of him and speak of him like this as the God of all grace? Oh to be a people known supremely for this—that we proclaim Jesus Christ; to be known for nothing else except glorying in the cross of our Lord Jesus Christ, by which we are crucified to the world and the world is crucified to us.

May this word of God be written into our hearts. Who is God? It is the greatest of all questions. Here is his description of himself. He is the God who did not spare his own Son but gave him up for us all. He will freely give us all things. May God write that truth into our lives!